Fanon and the 'rationality of revolt'

FANON

&

THE 'RATIONALITY OF REVOLT'

BREATH, LIFE, TIME

Nigel C. Gibson

Daraja Press

Ottawa

Published by Daraja Press

Thinking Freedom

https://darajapress.com

CC BY-NC 4.0: Nigel C. Gibson, 2020
This work is licensed under a Creative Commons Attribution-NonCommercial 4.0 International License.

Cover design: Kate McDonnell
Cover photo: Tony Webster.tony@tonywebster.com. "We revolt simply because for many reasons we can no longer breathe." .-Franz Fanon..Banner outside the Minneapolis Police Department fourth precinct following the officer-involved shooting of Jamar Clark on November 15, 2015.

Library and Archives Canada Cataloguing in Publication

Title: Fanon and the 'rationality of revolt: Breath, life, time / Nigel C Gibson.

Names: Gibson, Nigel C., author.

Description: Series statement: Thinking freedom series

Identifiers: Canadiana (print) 20200313738 | Canadiana (ebook) 20200313894 | ISBN 9781988832777 (softcover) | ISBN 9781988832784 (EPUB)

Subjects: LCSH: Fanon, Frantz, 1925-1961. | LCSH: Revolutions—Philosophy.

Classification: LCC JC491 .G53 2020 | DDC 303.6/4—dc23

Contents

Introduction	1
The Rationality of Revolt	3
Breath	8
Life	10
Time	12
Rethinking Everything	16
About the author	19

Introduction

Fanon's idea that the measure of time not be that of the moment but that of the rest of the world takes on urgent significance in this moment of global movements for Black Lives after the police murder of George Floyd.[1]

We inhabit extraordinary times: times in which we are acutely aware of the intensity of what revolutionary thinker Frantz Fanon called 'the glare of history's floodlights.' Around the world, the invisible becomes visible as the pandemic throws new light on old inequalities. From the United States to Brazil and South Africa, it is those who had already been rendered acutely vulnerable who are on the front lines.

And then there is the rebellion. The velocity and scale at which the revolt against police murder that began in Minnesota after the death of George Floyd on May 25, 2020, and moved throughout the US, and then other parts of the world, was astonishing. It was impossible to predict, but then, in retrospect, it is utterly predictable. As George Floyd's death became a nodal point, calling for action as well as rethinking and self-clarification, many were reminded of an observation attributed to Lenin—that 'there are weeks where decades happen.' What will happen next? How can we play a role in determining the future, making sure that these rebellions are not taken over and watered down, and realizing the systematic and truly human-centered transformations that people crave? Fanon offers us some important insights into these challenges as his dialectic of liberation becomes newly alive in moments like ours.

Thinking about this moment with Fanon, we need to be aware of continuities and discontinuities—or, as he puts it, opacities—between the ages. Fanon is always speaking to us, but often in ways we cannot hear. We have to work to listen to him and to understand the new contexts and meanings in relative opacity. It is this constant dialogue that helps illuminate the present and enables ongoing fidelity to Fanon's call in the conclusion of *The Wretched of the Earth*, the necessity to work out new concepts, 'for ourselves and for humanity.'

Notes

1. Some of the material in this pamphlet first appeared in the South African publication *New Frame* (https://www.newframe.com/combat-breathing-the-spirit-of-rebellion-in-the-usa/and https://www.newframe.com/fanon-and-the-rationality-of-revolt/).

The Rationality of Revolt

One of the concepts that is central to Fanon's thought is the idea of 'the rationality of revolt.' And the practice of engaging Fanon not only with revolt but also with revolt's reason or rationality defines a uniquely Fanonian dialectic. In the chapter entitled 'Medicine and Colonialism' in *A Dying Colonialism*, he connects hearing patients speak of their symptoms to hearing everyday resistances in daily life: 'It is necessary to analyse, patiently and lucidly, each one of *the reactions* of the colonized, and *every time we do not understand*, we must tell ourselves that we are at the heart of the drama, that of the *impossibility of finding a meeting ground in any colonial situation.*' In a racist society like the US, a similar situation occurs. In other words, understanding requires both careful and self-critical listening while maintaining an awareness of meaning and context. The important first step is to understand how reactions are not forced into a ready-made scenario.

For Fanon the hospital and the doctor's office are spaces of pathologization where the patients are therefore deemed irrational and thereby in need of being controlled (and medicated). In a racist society where white is considered the norm it is normal for the Black person to be abnormalized. The colonial regime and its institutions pathologizes the colonized as hysterical and thus for Fanon this has to be understood socially. Society, he says, is the source of the problem. Becoming more aware of institutional racism does not mean its dissolution and it is often forgotten how racism is internalized by those objectified by it and how resistance to institutional racism, to medicalization and to the fear of hospitals, for example, is considered irrational. All revolt is pathologized but for Fanon this resistance expresses an elemental rationality of revolt.

Politically, then, Fanon insists on self-critical reflection to enable listening as a first step towards understanding. It is on this basis of working with those who are considered external to history *and* rationality that new concepts are allowed room for their own development. Moreover, just as the hospital became the space of hearing reason in madness, the colony itself became the clinic for Fanon's praxis. The question is how to hear reason in revolt in these repressive spaces.

As stated above, understanding this reason requires both critical listening and the development of new ways of thinking through which to hear, with each dependent on the other. Listening, however, cannot begin without critique, and Fanon is utterly critical of what he calls the 'common opportunists' who simply repeat what they hear. To hear, in other words, means to engage critically. There is an important echo here of Gramsci's notion of the 'philosophy of praxis.' For Gramsci the philosophy of praxis had to become a 'consciousness full of contradictions,' that is to say, critically engaged with the revolt. It isn't enough to praise mass action but rather it is necessary to engage its contradictions and, Fanon argues, 'elevate this element to a principle of knowledge and action.'

In *The Wretched of the Earth*, Fanon connects this praxis to the idea of the rationality of revolt—a concept which becomes the new beginning that opens up both action and thought. For example, the current mass movement across professional sports and especially in the NBA and WNBA has transcended Colin Kaepernick's individual act of taking a knee and has given it a new and collective voice.

Fanon immediately adds a critique of the old leadership and old politics, and here he is speaking of the politicos who want to close down thinking into a series of reformist or even faux-revolutionary demands which are constructed by old concepts. In the US reformism often takes the form of the vote. Everything in this election year is being funneled into beating Trump. And while this is a minimum demand, it silences more radical demands and ignores the larger issue that we must face, namely, almost half the electorate has openly supported a white supremacist.

In contrast, real debates continue to take place, as Fanon insists, must take place, in the movements on the streets. And 'in defiance of those inside the movement who tend to think that [nuance and] shades of meaning constitute dangers and drive wedges into the solid block of popular opinion,' thinking becomes alive to action and principles are actually 'worked out' in the struggles for freedom.

In a context in which time speeds up and there are weeks where decades happen, a critique of time and the idea that we 'don't have time to discuss' is absolutely necessary when action demands more action. It often takes time to be inclusive and patient but this reflects a new form of political activity based on real action 'living inside history.' In this moment living inside history becomes alive with those who had been excluded from it and who become able to 'take the lead with their brains and their muscles in the fight for freedom.' But this cannot happen automatically. Fanon is aware of the weight of oppression. And thus the challenge for revolutionary intellectuals is to listen and to help work out the movement's own self-clarification, to help develop what the movement itself is revealing. As Fanon puts it, these 'unexpected facets

... bring out new meanings and *pinpoint the contradictions* camouflaged by these facts.'

For example, the fact of higher proportions of death from COVID 19 among Black and Brown people takes on a new meaning in the context of the movement for Black Lives. The high proportion of Black and Brown people working in low-paid, 'essential' jobs, living in crowded and cramped conditions, suffering from ill health now becomes seen as an expressions of systemic racism not of 'individual' choices. The idea of prison abolition connects not only with the demand for police abolition and the history of the police dating back to the days of slavery, but also with the contemporary history of mental health in the context of capitalism.

It is in the working out of these sometimes unexpected facets that Fanon's discussion takes on an important class dynamic. Whether they called themselves nationalists or socialists, the anticolonial national elite is unprepared, Fanon argues, because they lack practical ties with the movements from below. This disconnection expresses both a colonial mentality and a cowardice deriving, he argues, from their 'incapacity ... to *rationalize popular praxis, their incapacity* to attribute it any reason.' It betrays an elitist attitude toward mass action, which it considers ill-informed and tries to control or suppress. After gaining political independence, he sums up, this elite takes over the colonial state as its prize and continues on by other means: of exploitation, suppression, and necropolitics. In the "North Africa Syndrome" Fanon calls the experience a 'daily death.' The US prison-industrial complex, with its cycles of criminalization, incarceration, criminalization, and systemic racism is a clear example of what necropolitics means, especially in this moment of COVID-19.[1]

Notes

1. This system starts early. 42% of boys and 35% of girls in juvenile facilities are Black.

Breath

In the conclusion to his first book *Black Skin, White Masks*, Fanon writes that the Vietnamese revolted 'quite simply because it became impossible for them to breathe, in more than one sense of the word.' This quote quickly made it onto posters and social media after Eric Garner's murder in 2014[1] and again after George Floyd's cry for his mother, which resonated deeply around the world. 'I can't breathe' is literal—a response to the police and to a pandemic which attacks the lungs.

Fanon speaks of colonization and racism as the crushing of life and the denial of space, food, water, and air. In a colonial situation life is not perceived 'as flowering,' he writes, 'but as a permanent struggle against an omnipresent death' because 'there is not occupation of territory, on the one hand, and independence of persons on the other. It is the country as a whole, *its history, its daily pulsation* that are contested.' Under these conditions, breath itself is a threat: '*It is a combat breathing*.' The imagery is especially evocative in this moment—in more ways than one.

For Fanon, revolt is necessary to life; every breath is a combat breath, a challenge, and 'a clandestine form of existence.' This combat breath sanctions—'at whatever cost,' he adds in *The Wretched of the Earth*—the invasion of 'the enemy's fortress ...

endangering [its] 'security" and breeding fear into those forces. Combat breathing then becomes another history—a history in the making.

Old colonial and racist tropes are wheeled out, pacification takes place, and outsiders are blamed. But when history is moving and opening up, if only for a moment, what is the rationality of revolt? New meanings are brought out and old tropes are countered by participant narratives from the ground up, which quickly become shared: the Third Precinct of the Minneapolis police is the home of legal murder; the AFL-CIO is a representation of the police union; Target is what cannot be afforded. A week after the revolt began on May 25, 2020, it had become national. The sheer scale was historic, but what of the thinking and rationality of revolt? We should be skeptical of *a priori* meanings jamming the new into old categories. 'There is an *impossibility of finding a meeting ground*,' Fanon warns.

Notes

1. According to the *New York Times*, more than 40 people have been recorded being killed by police after warning, 'I can't breathe.' 'Three Words. 70 Cases. The Tragic History of 'I Can't Breathe.'"By Mike Baker, Jennifer Valentino-DeVries, Manny Fernandez and Michael LaForgia. See https://www.nytimes.com/interactive/2020/06/28/us/i-cant-breathe-police-arrest.html

Life

Breath is of course connected to life itself. Just a few pages earlier in *Black Skin, White Masks*, in his discussion of recognition, Fanon talks about forms of life. In the French colonies, he argues, when 'the white masters grudgingly [announced]' that 'slavery shall no longer exist ... The upheaval reached the Black from the outside.' They were acted upon by '*values that were not engendered by their actions.*' Thus, he says, they 'went from one way of life to another, *not from one life to another.*' Here, Fanon agrees with Hegel, whom he quotes: 'the essential nature of self-consciousness is not *bare existence, is not the merely immediate form* in which it at first makes its appearance, is not its mere absorption in the expanse of life.' Fanon then explains: 'I am not ... locked in thinghood.' To be thingified is to be depersonalized. '*I desire somewhere else and something* else.' Another life, something beyond 'bare existence.' And he demands 'that an account be taken of my contradictory activity insofar as I pursue *something other than life, insofar as I am fighting for the birth of a human world,* in other words, a world of reciprocal recognitions.'

He repeats this in *The Wretched of the Earth*, declaring that, under colonialism, 'living does not mean embodying a set of values, does not mean integrating oneself into the coherent, constructive development of a world.' To live simply means not to die. To exist means staying alive. 'Life can emerge only from the destruction of colonialism.' But, he warns, reactions against colonial Manicheanism must undergo a dialectical change or be doomed to repetition. The struggle must become a new way of life, not 'a type of freedom that does not get beyond an attitude of bondage,' as Hegel puts it. Fanon's analysis turns not only on struggle but also on the values of the struggle. This is a new, collective, thinking, combat breath. That is to say, whereas breathing itself is considered an act of resistance in the colonial world, in the struggle this combat breath becomes part of thinking and the collective action of the social movements.

Time

Hemmed in, crushed, denied space, food, and clean water, the powerful descriptions of colonial and racialized spaces in *The Wretched of the Earth*—and of the colonial world as a motionless world of statues—have rightly been considered one of Fanon's most important contributions. While space is absolutely essential to his analysis, so too is time. As he says in *Black Skin, White Masks*, 'the problem considered here is one of time.'

Fanon refuses to consider the present as definitive, and searches for glimpses of the future in the present. He phrases it wonderfully when he describes the Algerian revolution as being 'no longer in future heaven,' but present in the radical actions and consciousness of the people. The idea of future time being in the present is, in a sense, similar to Karl Marx's description of time as 'the space for human development.'

In *The Wretched of the Earth*, Fanon asks about the timing of revolt. 'In this atmosphere of violence ... which is just under the skin ... What makes the lid blow off?' It is impossible to predict but as we look back over the past few months and their concatenation of events, the reasons for why the revolt broke out seem obvious, though its mass character seems beyond everyone's expectations.

In *A Dying Colonialism*, Fanon explains the event as an opening into historical time—a time in which the oppressed become historical actors, and the future suddenly becomes a matter of contestation: 'Before the rebellion there was the life, the movement, the existence of the settler, and on the other side the continued agony of the colonized. Since 1954 ... in Algerian society, it seems, *things no longer repeat themselves as they did before.*' There is a new memory of the long resistance, a history recited and reclaimed by the youth. In Algeria of the mid 1950s this included the resistance to French colonialism from a hundred years earlier in which so-called pacification campaigns were realized by mass asphyxiation.[1]

Fanon dates the rebellion to November 1, 1954, the day that the National Liberation Front launched a number of attacks in Algeria against French colonial forces. For Fanon, it was an extraordinary declaration of intent against the odds that led to a radical change in consciousness among the colonized.

What becomes obvious on reflection is that the spontaneity of popular action is not simply spontaneous, but the result of ongoing thinking and organizing. When demonstrators in Bristol, England pulled down the statue of slave trader Edward Colston and dumped it in the same harbor where his slave ships used to dock, there was thinking—a rationality of revolt intimating a different world. When demonstrators deface the statues of 'national heroes' such as George Washington in the US and Winston Churchill in the UK, they express a moment of decolonization reminiscent of Fanon's opening pages in *The Wretched of the Earth*.

There, Fanon talks about another notion of time and dignity—one that is fully integrated with a conception of human life and one that humanizes and socializes the individual. Critical of the betrayal by the nationalist elites, he offers a different vision: that 'the yardstick of time must no longer be that of the moment or up till the next harvest, but must become that of the rest of the world.' In other words, Fanon is projecting a radically humanist conception of time, imagining another world which can be consciously built from below and already intimated in the thoughts and actions of the radical movements. He immediately links this to 'humanizing work.' Today, Fanon's idea of the 'rest of the world' takes on a significance that is universal and urgent in this moment of climate and global pandemic.

Fanon's yardstick is a notion of time as liberated from the colonial foreclosure of possibility and as separate from capitalist time dominated by dead labor. Time, instead, is connected with life, self-determination, and the development of a historical subjectivity that emerges through struggle. Nothing, however, is automatic. Fanon's notion of time is also extremely sensitive to the psychological situation that people find themselves in, including the weight of collective trauma and prospects for future health that only time, he says, will fully reveal. There are no guarantees of recovery but time, of course, has to become consciously human time. It has to become the time for health and the recovery of those knowingly and unknowingly traumatized and broken down by colonialism. He is aware that the process of creating actional people liberated from internalized inferiority might take time, insisting that there is no magical process, no leader, no other who will do it for us. For Fanon, the absolute negativity of colonialism and racism, the dual movement of uprooting the old society and creating the new, requires the revolutionary movement to continue after its initial victory. Reforms are not enough and Fanon is dismissive of the idea that the colonial system can be taken over and used for progressive purposes. He quotes Marx in the conclusion to *Black Skin, White Masks:* The revolution 'cannot draw its poetry from the past.' Human liberation necessitates the continuation of the revolution from below in all social relations.

In a certain way, you could say this way of taking measure of time echoes Marx's idea of time and his critique of capitalism's commodification and disposal of human time. What is time for capitalism but opportunity for profit? In *Grundrisse,* Marx contrasts a struggle over time and labor (forced and free), understanding a wholly different and more freely associated notion of labor. By freely associated Marx means not based on '*direct* forced labor, slavery, or *indirect* forced labor, wage *labour*.' Marx highlights the actions of the free Blacks in Jamaica who only produce what is strictly necessary for their own consumption as a rational and elemental resistance to capitalism. It is not that they have intentionally rejected commodity culture, but rather that they exhibit a fundamental understanding of capitalism: that 'capital does not exist as capital, because autonomous wealth as such can exist only either on the basis of *direct* forced labour, slavery, or *indirect* forced labour, wage *labour*.' And they refuse to go along with it.[2]

Notes

1. Combat breathing is reminiscent of General Bugeaud's boast from the 1840s on which French settler colonialism is built: 'I have all the exits hermetically sealed and I make a huge cemetery.' It is important to remember the reactionary colonial character of the liberal de Tocqueville's support for settler colonialism in Algeria and his support of Bugeaud's methods of annihilation. See Losurdo Liberalism: A Counter History (New York: Verso, 2011) p. 236
2. In the *Grundrisse* Marx writes with glee about an article in *The Times* of London about the cry of outrage of a West Indian plantation owner at the free Blacks of Jamaica, who 'do not care a damn for the sugar and the fixed capital invested in the plantations, but rather observe the planters' impending bankruptcy with an ironic grin of malicious pleasure.'

Rethinking Everything

Fanon sustains a fundamental sense of movement and opening to the future in the form of a critical, questioning mode of praxis. He concludes his first book, *Black Skin, White Masks*, with a prayer: 'O my body, make of me always a man who questions!'

Fanon's final text, *The Wretched of the Earth*, includes a radical questioning which comes from within the revolutionary movement. At one point he writes, 'perhaps we need to rethink everything.' Such a total rethinking seems remarkable on the eve of victory against the French after a long and exhausting war of liberation. Yet, for Fanon, the need for a second revolution is necessary and consistent with his idea that principles continue to be 'worked out' inside the struggles for freedom. The future as a 'limitless humanity' is connected to new ways of life that must guard against the 'brutality of thought.' Fanon's openness to the idea of a total and intentional transformation of social relations continues in an anticapitalist ecological frame: 'Perhaps it's necessary to begin everything all over again: to change the nature of the country's exports ... to re-examine the soil and mineral resources, the rivers and—why not —the sun's productivity.' The ecological dimension here is essential to human life and dignity and expresses what the struggle is really about.[1] Based on uprooting the alienated social relations of a racist and colonized society, reaching toward what Fanon calls a new humanism has to include everyone and rethinking everything. He immediately connects this ecological rethinking to the conditions of labor. 'If conditions of work are not modified,' he argues, 'centuries will be needed to humanize this world which has been forced down to animal level by imperial powers.' He's talking about the forms of forced and sweated labor called freedom in neoliberal and neocolonial capitalism that consume life and environments. In this extraordinary moment of global rebellion in the time of COVID-19, we know very well that we no longer have centuries. The time, as Fanon would have it, is now.

Notes

1. Fanon concludes *The Wretched of the Earth* arguing, 'this new humanity cannot do otherwise than define a new humanism both for itself and for others. It is prefigured in the objectives and methods of the conflict,' while Europe talks of humanism yet 'murder human beings everywhere they find them.' David Walker's *Appeal to the Colored Citizens of the World*, (1829) makes a similar point, 'Compare your own language ... extracted from your Declaration of Independence, with your cruelties and murders inflicted by your cruel and unmerciful fathers and yourselves on our fathers and on us—men who have never given your fathers or you the least provocation.'

About the author

Nigel C. Gibson is author of *Fanon: The Postcolonial Imagination* (2003, Arabic translation, 2013), and *Fanonian Practices in South Africa: From Steve Biko to Abahlali baseMjondolo* (2011) and he is the co-author with Robert Beneduce of *Frantz Fanon, Psychiatry and Politics* (2017). He is currently working on an edited collection to be published by Daraja Press on the sixtieth anniversary of *The Wretched of the Earth* in 2021. His two earlier edited collections on Fanon are *Rethinking Fanon: The Continuing Dialogue* (1999) and *Living Fanon: Global Perspectives* (2011). He teaches at Emerson College in Boston.

www.ingramcontent.com/pod-product-compliance
Lightning Source LLC
Chambersburg PA
CBHW071729020426
42333CB00017B/2456